Paws In
The Moment

52 ways to
embrace mindfulness
with your dog

Vicki Jurica

ISBN: 979-8-9917771-0-0 (paperback)

ISBN: 979-8-9917771-1-7 (digital)

Reviews for *Paws in the Moment*

"I love this book. I'm an animal communicator and see the spiritual side of our animal friends and how it intersects in our lives with them. This book takes a physical action and includes a spiritual journey with the action. It doesn't get any better than that when you're with your animal friend. I intend to recommend this book to all of my doggie clients."

~ Ashara Morris, Animal Communicator, Author and Gestaltist

"We live in a fast-paced world where focusing on being present and self-care usually falls to the bottom of the list. One impact is not spending enough time nourishing the relationship with our canine companions. Vicki provides opportunities to release the tensions of everyday life, honor the needs and sentience of "man's best friend," and ways to create healthy relationships that could also translate to our human counterparts."

~ BB Harding, Human Design specialist, Coach and Author

"We all love our dogs — and I don't know a single dog owner who doesn't want to have a better relationship with their companion. Vicki's book takes us through a year's worth of simple, easy-to-accomplish, relationship building experiences that both deepen the time spent with our canine companions and allow us to form a better connection with our inner selves. Highly recommend."

~ Kim Beer, Rancher, former working dog breeder, and Gestaltist

"I've followed Vicki Jurica's work for a long time, and one thing is certain: she practices what she preaches. Mindfulness is a way of life for Vicki, and she also possesses the rare understanding of the obstacles that often get in the way. 'Paws in The Moment' is a game changer for dog lovers- grab your copy today!"

~ Amy Butler Angell, LPC

Dedication

To dogs everywhere. You show up in our lives, step forward in welcoming friendship and show us how to live in the moment with love and joy. Thank you.

Autumn 2013 -2024

Acknowledgments

No book is published by itself. There's a whole group of folks that joined me on this journey. ABA, your constant presence in my life has been a light that I use as my guide; KB, your generosity, wisdom and friendship creates ripples that will touch the world. BH, your endless curiosity opens my world in wonderful ways. To AS, AM, and my Scribes writing group thank you for the support and the accountability. To my family - surprise! I wrote a book. And finally, to the dogs in my life, thank you for reminding me to be right here, right now. I am blessed.

Contents

The intention of this book is to build a deeper relationship with yourself and your dog, not put undue stress upon your relationship. Listen to your body and your dog. Adjust any activity listed as needed. Please follow leash laws and pick up after your dog

Forward: Understanding Mindfulness

In today's fast-paced world, the concept of mindfulness is often mentioned, yet its deeper meaning and transformative potential are sometimes overlooked. Mindfulness is more than living in the present moment. It is an invitation to turn inward and explore the rich landscape of our inner world. True mindfulness asks us to pause and gently inquire: What am I thinking? What am I feeling? How is my energy responding to this moment? Where do I feel it in my body? And to do all of this without judgment, simply observing and accepting the moment for what it is.

Mindfulness also expands our awareness beyond the boundaries of ourselves. It encourages us to recognize our deep interconnectedness with all living beings and the world around us. As we nurture this understanding, our gratitude, compassion, and empathy naturally grow. We begin to see that every breath, every emotion, every interaction holds the potential for connection and transformation.

Throughout this journey, we are guided by the practice of **PAWS:**

- **P** - pause and come to stillness
- **A** - air — take a deep, slow breath
- **W** - wonder about our inner experience (thoughts, feelings, reactions) and what's happening around us
- **S** - step forward with greater awareness and information

This simple yet profound process invites us to live with conscious intention, creating space for deeper understanding and meaningful action.

Mindful living is an active process—one that requires ongoing attention, curiosity, and care. It is a practice of tuning in, expanding out, and walking through life with both presence and purpose. Through the unconditional love and innate wisdom of our dogs, we are gently reminded to return to ourselves, to listen, and to live each moment with an open and compassionate heart.

Introduction: The Wisdom of Dogs — A Path to Awareness and Mindful Living

Our dogs are more than companions — they are wise, loving teachers. In their presence, we are invited into stillness, authenticity, and deeper awareness. They reflect back our truest selves, offering sanctuary, acceptance, and gentle reminders to return to the present moment. When we open ourselves to the lessons they offer, we naturally begin to cultivate mindfulness, emotional awareness, and personal growth.

Unconditional Acceptance and Support

Dogs greet us each day with open hearts and no judgment. They don't care about our mistakes, the masks we wear, or the chaos we sometimes carry. They simply see us — and love us, exactly as we are. Their acceptance is rare and profound, and when we let it in, it gently teaches us to extend that same kindness to ourselves and others.

Understanding and Forgiveness

Scold your dog, and moments later they're by your side, tail wagging, love still shining. Dogs don't hold grudges — they forgive freely, love openly, and move on with grace. In their way, they show us that letting go, offering second chances, and softening around imperfection is a path to deeper connection.

Expanding Emotional Awareness and Intelligence

Dogs feel deeply. They sense our emotions before we speak them, often before we fully feel them ourselves. Their quiet empathy invites us to tune in — to notice what's stirring within, and to respond with gentleness. Through them, we begin to better understand our own emotional landscape and build resilience from the inside out.

Compassion and Empathy

Caring for a dog nurtures something tender in us. We learn to listen with our whole selves — to respond to their needs with presence and love. This deepens our ability to be compassionate not just toward our dogs, but toward all beings.

Understanding Non-Verbal Communication

Dogs speak with more than sound — they use energy, posture, movement, and presence. When we slow down and observe, we begin to "hear" them more clearly. In doing so, we also become more attuned to the non-verbal language in the human world, allowing us to connect and relate more deeply across all relationships.

Self-Responsibility and Ownership

Being in relationship with a dog invites us to show up — consistently, honestly, and with care. Dogs respond to our energy, mirroring our emotional state back to us. Their presence holds us accountable, nudging us toward greater awareness of how we affect those around us. In this, we are reminded to walk with intention and integrity.

Focus, Concentration, and Learning

Training a dog requires us to be clear, present, and patient. We learn to communicate in small, manageable steps. Along the way, we refine our focus, adaptability, and understanding — not just with our dogs, but in all areas of our lives.

Movement, Strength, and Vitality

Dogs get us moving — out the door, into nature, and back into our bodies. Whether it's a walk around the block or a romp at the park, their enthusiasm for movement helps us reconnect with our own. In meeting their need for activity, we nourish our own vitality and well-being.

Exploring the World with Awe and Wonder

To walk beside a dog is to see the world anew.
Every scent, breeze, and rustle of leaves becomes
something to notice and explore. Dogs remind us
that there is still wonder all around us — if we
take the time to notice.

Opportunities for Play and Joy

Dogs are masters of joy. Whether it's a game of
tug, a goofy grin, or a full-speed zoomie in the
yard, they teach us how to play again. In their
world, the present moment is enough — and in
joining them, we rediscover that same lightness
and laughter within ourselves.

Living in the Present Moment

Dogs don't dwell on the past or worry about the
future. They live here, now — fully engaged in
the moment. Their ability to be present reminds
us that peace and contentment are always
available when we return to this breath, this step,
this moment.

Walking the Path Together

This journey with your dog is about more than care and companionship. It's a path toward mindful, intentional living — a way of moving through the world with awareness, presence, and gratitude. They are not just by your side. They are your guide, your mirror, your reminder of what truly matters.

Mindful living with your dog isn't about grand practices — it's found in the small, sacred moments you share each day. These moments are your invitation to slow down, breathe deep, and open your heart. With your dog's wisdom and love, you'll find yourself more grounded, more present, and more deeply connected to the beauty of your life.

This is your invitation to go deeper into the everyday moments you already share. Each simple activity — a walk, a cuddle, a stretch, a nap — becomes a chance to slow down, connect, and *PAWS*. These practices aren't about adding more to your life, but about noticing what's already there — the richness, the beauty, the presence your dog embodies so effortlessly. Together, you and your dog can move through each week with deeper connection, grounded presence, and a renewed sense of wonder for the life you're living side by side.

Anywhere Activities

Designed for any setting, these activities
invite you and your dog to slow down,
tune in, and embrace the moment –
wherever you happen to be.

When I look into the
eyes of an animal,
I do not see an
animal,
I see a living being.
I see a soul.
I feel a friend.
~ Anthony Douglas
Williams

I See You

What you need: You and your dog.

What to Do: Make eye contact with your dog. Look at your dog to See them.

The Invitation: One of the simplest mindfulness practices you can share with your dog is to truly see them. Not a glance or a distracted pat, but a quiet, intentional pause to meet their gaze. Sit together. Soften your focus. Look into the loyal, loving soul beside you.

Life moves quickly. We often rush past those who share our days without really noticing. But mindfulness asks us to slow down. Your dog does this naturally. They see you — tired, joyful, or hurting — and greet you without judgment.

When you meet your dog's eyes with presence, you honor their spirit and your bond. Whisper *"I see you,"* and let it remind you to acknowledge not only your dog, but everyone you share your life with. In those small, mindful moments, deeper connection grows — with your dog, yourself, and the world around you.

What do you notice as you acknowledge your dog in this way?

**Yoga is a journey
of the self,
through the self,
to the self.**
~ The Bhagavad Gita

Yoga with Your Dog

What You Need: You, your dog, yoga mat.

What to Do: Let your dog enhance your awareness as you practice a simple yoga routine.

The Invitation: Yoga invites you to slow down, connect your breath with your body, and return your attention inward. With mindful movement, you create space to notice, feel, and listen to your body's quiet wisdom. Yoga strengthens not just muscles and flexibility, but the vital bridge between mind and body.

As you practice, you'll experience greater clarity, balance, and connection — not only within yourself, but with the world around you. Breathwork teaches you to shift your energy through intentional breathing. Dogs naturally mirror this self-regulation, breathing calmly when at ease.

When you invite your dog to join you on the mat, you share more than a practice. You build new pathways in your brain, strengthen your bond, and celebrate the simple joy of being fully present — together. Stretch, breathe, and grow side-by-side, nurturing your mind, body, spirit.

What do you notice as you do yoga with your dog? How do they participate with you?

Play is the highest form of research.
~ Albert Einstein

Play Time

What you Need: You, your dog and a toy or game.

What to Do: Play with your dog, undistracted.

The Invitation: As adults, play often slips to the bottom of our lists, crowded out by tasks and obligations. Yet play is not a luxury — it's essential. It soothes the mind, lifts the spirit, and opens the door to creativity and imagination.

When you play with your dog — tug, chase, or a food scatter — you tap into a shared language of joy and connection. Play builds trust, strengthens relationships, and reminds us that life is meant to be enjoyed.

Dogs stay rooted in their sense of play, moving freely, and celebrating the simple pleasure of being alive. When we join them, we reconnect with spontaneity, laughter, and the beauty of the present moment.

Through playful moments, we weave stronger bonds, nurture empathy, and remember what it feels like to be lighthearted, open, and fully here.

What do you notice within you as you play with your dog?

**Grooming is not just
about appearance,
it's about well-being.**
~ Unknown

Mindful Grooming

What you need: You, your dog and grooming tools.

What to Do: Groom your dog slowly and mindfully.

The Invitation: Grooming is more than keeping clean — it's a natural act of connection. In both human and animal groups, grooming deepens bonds, builds trust, and offers a quiet moment of caring.

When you gently brush your dog, you're not just tending to their coat. You tune into their body language, notice their boundaries, and listen with your hands and heart. Allow your dog to sniff and explore the tools you use. This simple act of respect and curiosity reassures them and strengthens your relationship.

The slow, rhythmic motion of brushing becomes its own meditation — calming your mind, grounding your energy, and creating a peaceful space for both of you. trust, and deep connection.

How does the chore of grooming change when you shift to honor this form of caring?

Joy is best
when shared—
just ask two dogs
at play.
~ Unknown

Doggy Playdate

What you need: You, your dog and their fur friend and safe place for them to play.

What to Do: Arrange a playdate for your dog and observe their interactions.

The Invitation: Play isn't just fun — it's necessary. Setting up a doggy playdate gives your dog the gift of connecting dog to dog, romping, and communicating in ways only they can.

As they chase, tug, and bow into playful invitations, you have the chance to simply watch. Notice the dance of body language — the turns they take, the breaks they honor, the joy they share without a single word. Silent observation becomes a mindfulness practice all its own. By staying present, you deepen your understanding of how your dog thinks, feels, and connects.

Playdates aren't just for your dog's happiness — they open new doorways of trust, empathy, and connection for both of you. Through play, you're reminded that sometimes the purest communication happens without a word.

How would being aware of your own body language improve the relationships in your life?

**Happiness is a
picnic with
your best friend.**
~ Your dog

Picnic Time

What you need: You, your dog, dog safe foods and picnic blanket.

What to Do: Pack a picnic for you and your dog.

The Invitation: Sharing a meal has long been a way to deepen companionship and connection. A simple picnic with your dog — a basket filled with dog-friendly treats like turkey, cheese, apples— becomes a shared experience of joy.

As you sit together outdoors, let your senses open. Notice the sights, sounds, and smells around you. Let your dog lead your awareness — they'll notice details you might otherwise miss, drawing you more deeply into the moment.

Settling in side-by-side, and sharing simple foods fosters relaxation, gratitude, and presence. It's not about doing anything grand — it's about being together, savoring the simple pleasures of nature, companionship, and a quiet meal shared in trust and love.

What do you notice as you share this experience with your dog?

**Breath is the bridge
which connects life to
consciousness.**
~ Thich Nhat Hanh

Breathwork

What You Need: You and your dog.

What to Do: Sit calmly with your dog and practice deep breathing.

The Invitation: Breath is your quiet companion — a bridge between your inner world and the life around you. Though it happens without thought, breath can also be shaped with intention, guiding you back to calm.

Sit with your dog. Feel the rise and fall of their breath. Let your own breathing slow to match theirs — easy, natural, steady. In this quiet rhythm, you both find a deeper presence.

Dogs instinctively regulate their emotions through breath. When you become aware of their patterns and your own, you get a glimpse of both of your inner landscapes — your tension, your ease, your readiness to return to balance.

Breathwork reminds you: while you can't control every moment, you can choose how you meet it.

How does you and your dog's breath shift throughout the day?

Those who were seen
dancing were thought
to be insane by those
who could not hear
the music.
~ Friedrich Nietzsche

Dancing with Your Dog

What You Need: You, your dog and music.

What to Do: Put on music and move freely with your dog.

The Invitation: Dancing is a celebration — a joyful way to move, laugh, and let go. Whether your steps are quick and playful or slow and flowing, dance shifts your energy and reconnects you to your body.

Turn on the music and invite your dog to join you. Spin, sway, bounce — let the rhythm pull you both into the moment. Follow their movements or create a simple routine together, building communication through shared steps and smiles.

Dancing strengthens muscles, opens flexibility, and invites pure, uncomplicated joy. It reminds you that connection isn't always serious — sometimes it's found in silly spins, shared laughter, and wiggling tails. In dancing with your dog, you don't just move your body — you move your heart, right into the present moment, where joy lives.

As you dance around, how do you and your dog's energies shift and expand?

Obstacles are those frightful things you see when you take your eyes off the goal.
~ Henry Ford

Create a Dog Obstacle Course

What You Need: You, your dog, and household items like a broom, boxes, and furniture.

What to Do: Set up a simple obstacle course in your living room or yard for your dog.

The Invitation: Building a dog obstacle course is an act of creativity and play. A broom laid across chairs becomes a jump, a bench transforms into a balance beam, and an open-ended box becomes a tunnel of adventure.

Setting up a course invites both you and your dog into physical and mental engagement. As you guide them through each section, you strengthen communication, trust, and teamwork — celebrating every leap, weave, and joyful dash.

Delight grows in the shared experience. Every obstacle offers a chance to encourage, support, and cheer each other on. The course itself becomes a beautiful metaphor: life isn't just about reaching the end but enjoying the journey.

What's it like to create a fun course and both of you successfully complete it?

Music expresses that which cannot be said and on which it is impossible to be silent.
~ Victor Hugo

Sing to Your Dog

What you need: You and your dog.

What to Do: Sing or hum a soft melody while petting or hanging out with your dog.

The Invitation: Singing with your dog is pure magic — a joyful way to connect heart to heart. Every song, every silly note deepens the bond between you.

Crooning a lullaby during cuddle time, howling at the moon together, or cranking the radio on a joyride — it all weaves memories built on sound, laughter, and love. Your dog doesn't care if you can carry a tune. They know and cherish the music of your voice.

Singing lifts the spirit, sparks smiles and anchors you fully in the present moment. It invites spontaneity, playfulness, and celebration.

So sing your heart out. Make up songs, howl along, or dance and sway to your favorite beat. The joy is not in how perfect the song sounds — it's in the feeling you share when you sing it together.

What thoughts and feelings do you notice as you sing to your dog?

Sometimes, all you
need is the breeze and
a moment of peace.
~ Unknown

Enjoy the Breeze Together

What You Need: You, your dog and an open window or an outdoor space.

What to Do: Sit with your dog in an area where you can feel the breeze.

The Invitation: Close your eyes. Feel the breeze brush against your skin. In this simple, quiet moment, you are invited to pause, to notice, to be fully present.

Watch the easy dance of nature — the wind slipping through the leaves, twisting and turning with grace. Listen to the soft tinkling of wind chimes carried by the air. Lift your nose, just like your dog does, and breathe deep. Notice the scents riding the breeze — how many can you recognize?

Feel the gentle flutter of your hair, the soft tug on your clothes, the kiss of coolness on your face. Let the wind wrap you in its quiet song.

In the easy, steady companionship of your dog, simply *be*. Let the world blow by you while you stay anchored in this one, beautiful moment — connected by breath, breeze, and companionship.

What do you notice when you observe the breeze through your senses?

**The best way to
understand someone
is to walk a mile in
their shoes.**
~ Unknown

Shadow Your Dog

What You Need: You and your dog.

What to Do: Spend time following your dog around your house and yard.

The Invitation: Follow your dog through their day. No guiding, no directing — simply observe.

Watch their choices, their interests, their reactions. Notice how they move through familiar spaces, what draws their attention, how their body language shifts moment to moment. This is an active practice of listening without words, of being fully present to another's experience.

By shadowing your dog, you begin to see the world through their eyes — discovering small wonders, quiet habits, and unspoken rhythms you might have missed. You are invited to step out of your own perspective and into theirs.

With this gentle attention, empathy and compassion naturally grow. You connect more deeply, not by changing anything, but simply by noticing — and honoring — the life moving right beside you.

What comes into your awareness as you view the world through your dog's perspective

**Patience is not the
ability to wait,
but the ability to keep
a good attitude while
waiting.**
~ Joyce Meyer

Mindful Waiting

What you need: You, your dog, and moment where you must "wait" for something.

What to Do: While waiting (for food, to go outside at a crosswalk, etc) remain present.

The Invitation: Waiting is a skill — one that both you and your dog can learn and grow into together.

Mindful waiting transforms idle moments into invitations for awareness. Instead of filling the space with impatience, you simply *witness* — allowing the moment to be exactly as it is, without rushing or resistance.

Notice how, once your dog learns to "wait," they stay present. They trust the moment, sensing when it's time to move and when it's time to pause. In following their lead, you also practice responding instead of reacting.

Mindful waiting deepens your awareness, strengthens patience, and nurtures gratitude for what *is*, not just what's next. In stillness, in quiet observation, the world unfolds — and you are there, fully present to witness it.

How can you stay more present during times of waiting? What would you notice?

**Home is
where my dog is.**
~ Every dog guardian

Your Dog's Favorite Spot

What You Need: You and your dog.

What to Do: Observe where your dog naturally gravitates when they want to relax.

The Invitation: Every dog has a special place — a quiet retreat where their body softens, and their spirit feels safe.

Find where your dog naturally drifts when they seek rest. Sit beside them. Feel the textures under your hand, notice the play of light and shadow, the warmth or coolness of the space. Listen to the stillness your dog has chosen.

Be curious. What makes this spot feel right to them? Do they tuck themselves into a quiet corner, or stretch out where life hums around them?

In noticing, you deepen your understanding. You learn not only where your dog feels at home, but how to better meet their needs for comfort, safety, and peace. Through these small acts of awareness, you also expand your capacity to offer kindness – honoring your dog in your life.

Where are your dog's favorite spots to relax? Can you describe why they love it so much?

Almost everything
will work again if
you unplug it for a
few minutes...
including you.
~ Anne Lamont

"Do Nothing" Together

What You Need: You and your dog.

What to Do: Spend a chunk of time just hanging out with your dog, without distractions or plans.

The Invitation: Let your dog lead the way. Nap, lounge, snack, and move only when it feels right. Allow yourself to completely unwind, listening to your body's needs just as your dog naturally does. They are masters of the art of Being — fully present, fully connected to themselves and the world around them.

Disconnect from distractions. Sit together in quiet companionship. Feel your body soften, your breath slow, your mind grows silent. Notice how awareness sharpens in stillness. The colors around you seem brighter, the sounds clearer, the connection deeper.

By practicing the simple art of doing nothing, you strengthen your ability to meet each moment with full presence — responding to life not with urgency, but with gentle, grounded intention.

Sometimes, the greatest gift you can give yourself — and your dog — is simply to *Be*.

How is it to simply be present with your dog?

A dog's heartbeat is
the best kind of
rhythm.
~ Unknown

Heartbeats

What You Need: You, your dog and quiet place to rest with your dog.

What to Do: Lie with your dog and listen to the steady rhythm of their heartbeat.

The Invitation: Snuggle close to your dog and listen. Feel the steady rhythm of their heartbeat, a quiet song of life and presence.

Rest your head against their chest or hold them close and let them rest against yours. Let the moment unfold without rush — only breath, warmth, and the gentle thrum of connection.

Notice what stirs within you. What feelings arise when you slow down enough to listen?

Gently pet your dog, allowing love and gratitude to flow freely between you. In this quiet exchange, walls fall away. There is only presence, safety, and the deep comfort of shared life. In this moment, there is no past, no future — just you and your dog.

How does your entire being respond when you listen to your dog's heartbeat?

Camping with a dog
is the perfect
reminder that the best
moments in life don't
need WiFi.
~ Unknown

Camping With Your Dog

What You Need: You, your dog and camping gear or inside fort.

What to Do: Plan a camping trip with your dog or recreate the experience in your home.

The Invitation: Adventure begins the moment you step beyond your routine — tent packed or blankets draped in a homemade campsite.

With your dog by your side, embrace the spirit of exploration. Laugh, play, and stay flexible as you create memories stitched into the present moment.

Share dog-friendly foods, wander trails, tug and tumble, or curl up for flashlight-lit stories. As night falls, welcome the quiet. Notice how you and your dog naturally ease from day into night. If you're outdoors, breathe in the cool air, listen to the night sounds, feel the world shifting around you. If you're indoors, let imagination carry you into adventure.

Notice how your dog embraces it all — the journey, the laughter, the quiet — simply because they are with you.

What feeling, sensations and thoughts do you notice while doing this adventure with your dog?

One, two, three, cheese!
~All photographers everywhere

Photos With Your Dog

What You Need: You, your dog and camera/phone.

What to Do: Take photos of your dog in various poses, activities or locations.

The Invitation: Take photos of your dog — not for perfection, but for presence. Focus on capturing their spirit: the sparkle in their eyes, the playful tilt of their head, the quiet look of pure love.

Let your dog remind you how beautiful authenticity is.They express their feelings freely — excitement, curiosity, contentment — without concern for appearances.

As you photograph them, notice how they move through the world — fully present, fully themselves. Each image becomes a memory, a small celebration of the life you share.

Fill your phone, your heart, and your days with moments that matter — muddy paws, sideways glances, sleepy snuggles. In recording their story, you deepen your love and gratitude for this chapter of your journey together.

What's your emotional response to the photos of you and your dog?

Movement is a medicine for creating change in a person's physical, emotional and mental states.
~ Carol Welch

Exercise Together

What You Need: You, your dog, comfortable clothes and an open space.

What to Do: Choose a form of exercise that feels good for both you and your dog.

The Invitation: Your body — and your dog's — needs daily movement. But exercise isn't about pushing limits. It's a celebration of what you can do together. Start slow. Listen to your body and your dog's energy. Move as partners, connected and attuned.

Exercise strengthens more than muscles. It sharpens focus, lifts emotional well-being, increases flexibility, and builds resilience. As you move, you release stress and tension, strengthening both mind and body through connection.

Your dog becomes your accountability partner — eager, joyful, and fully present. They benefit just as you do: feeling stronger, happier, more alive. Exercise together invites mindfulness into motion. It asks you to stay aware, engaged, and grateful for the body that carries you, and the companion who runs beside you.

What changes do you notice within yourself and your dog when you exercise together?

**The expert in
anything was
once a beginner.**
~ Helen Hayes

Beginner's Mind

What You Need: You, your dog, patience and a sense of humor.

What to Do: Pick a new skill or trick that feels exciting but achievable for the both of you.

The Invitation: Stepping into something new means stepping into wonder — the open-hearted, curious energy of a beginner.

When you and your dog learn together, it's not about getting it perfect. It's about clear communication, patience, and a whole lot of laughter. Mistakes? They're just part of the adventure. Break new skills into small, easy steps. Celebrate every tiny success — wagging tails, happy dances, and all.

Watch your dog's approach: they leap into learning with joy, energy, and no fear of getting it wrong. They celebrate the journey, not just the goal. Follow their lead. Let excitement, humor, and curiosity guide you. Learning becomes less about mastering a skill and more about sharing smiles, building trust, and creating memories.

In a beginner's mind, every moment is fresh and full of possibility — and more fun together.

What additional awareness have you learned?

Inside Activities

These indoor activities are designed to bring mindfulness into your everyday routine. Within the comfort of your home, you and your dog can deepen your connection and calmness.

**Silence isn't empty,
it's full of answers.**
~ Any Mindfulness
teacher

Doggie Meditation

What You Need: You and your dog in a quiet setting.

What to Do: Your dog becomes the center of your meditation.

The Invitation: Quietly sit beside them and pause. Gently use all your senses to connect. Notice their slow, steady breathing.

Look — nose to tail. See the color of their eyes, the way their fur grows, the soft curl of a smile.

Touch — run your fingers through their fur, feel the velvet of their ears, the tickle of their whiskers.

Listen — match your breath with theirs.
Hear the sounds that are uniquely *them* — the sighs, the snuffles, the quiet heartbeats.

Smell — bury your face in their fur and breathe in the scent of home.

Kiss — a gentle kiss on their forehead, a thank you for being exactly who they are.

Notice what rises within you.

Food is symbolic of love when words are inadequate.
~ Alan D. Wolfelt

Mindful Mealtime

What You Need: You, your dog and their favorite meal.

What to Do: Observe you dog at mealtime.

The Invitation: Turn mealtime into a mindful ritual by staying with your dog as they eat. Instead of setting the bowl down and moving on, pause. Sit nearby. Be present. Watch how your dog approaches their food — do they dive in with excitement or nibble with quiet care? Notice their body language — the wag of a tail, the sparkle in their eyes, the simple joy of being nourished.

Sharing in their moment of gratitude invites you to your own. A silent thanks for the food, for their companionship, for this ordinary, beautiful moment.

Mindful mealtime deepens your connection — to your dog, to the act of caring, and to the rhythm of daily life. In slowing down, you discover that even the smallest routines can be filled with presence, joy, and love.

What do you notice about mealtime? How can you make it more meaningful for the two of you?

**Book are a uniquely
portable magic.**
~ Stephen King

Read Together

What You Need: You, your dog, a good book and cozy spot.

What to Do: Read your book aloud while sitting with your dog.

The Invitation: Reading offers a gentle pause — a break from the noise of the day and a doorway into new worlds. Snuggle in with your dog, book in hand. Let the words carry you to far-off places, introduce you to new characters, and spark imagination, empathy, and wonder.

Read aloud and bring your dog along for the journey. They'll listen without judgment, soothed by the rhythm of your voice — their favorite sound in the world. Maybe they drift into sleep, curled beside you in perfect peace.

In this shared quiet, you find connection — to the story, to yourself, and to the warm, steady presence at your side. Reading together becomes more than a pastime. It's a ritual of rest, a way to slow down, breathe deep, and simply *be*.

How does your focus on the book shift when you read to your dog?

Savor the moment.

~ Unknown

Chew Toy Time

What You Need: You, your dog and chewy toy.

What to Do: Give your dog a chew toy or treat.

The Invitation: Chewing is a natural, joyful behavior for dogs. Offer your dog a chew toy and slow down. Sit with them. Be present.

Watch as they focus completely on their treat — the way they hold it between their paws, the steady rhythm of their chewing, the small sounds of satisfaction that fill the air. Notice their body language — the relaxed tail, the soft gaze, the quiet joy of being fully absorbed in the moment.

Stay with them. Let their simple, pure enjoyment draw you deeper into your own awareness. Chew toy time becomes an invitation to practice patience, to notice the details, to feel gratitude for the small, beautiful moments you share.

In being fully present for your dog's happiness, you nurture not only their well-being — but your own.

How does your dog express their enjoyment of this experience? What comes up for you?

Touch has a memory.
~ John Keats

Mindful Touch

What You Need: You and your dog in a quiet spot.

What to Do: Gently pet your dog.

The Invitation: Touch is a language of love — a way both humans and dogs quietly say, *I'm here with you.* Sit beside your dog and gently lay your hand on them. With each stroke, let your affection flow through your fingers — a silent offering of love, gratitude. Two souls simply *being* together.

Notice how your dog responds. Honor their choices — whether they lean in for more or quietly shift away. A gentle pat on the head, a slow rub down the back, a good-natured scratch at the base of the tail — all simple acts that comfort you both.

Dogs, too, speak through touch — a paw resting on your arm, a soft lean into your body, a nudge of the nose. Through these moments, support and care pass back and forth, weaving an invisible bond.

What comes into your awareness as you gently pet your dog?

**Gratitude turns what
we have into enough.**
~ Unknown

Daily Gratitude

What You Need: You and your dog.

What to Do: Sit quietly with your dog and talk about all the things you're thankful for.

The Invitation: Gratitude gently shifts your focus — from what's missing to what's here. A daily practice helps you see the gifts already present, waiting to be noticed.

Sit with your dog and speak your gratitude aloud. Thank them for their presence, the lessons you've learned together, the comfort they bring, and the love that never wavers.

They may not understand every word, but they *feel* your intention. They sense it in your tone, your energy, your touch. They know they matter.

This simple act deepens your connection — not just with your dog, but with the world around you. Gratitude softens the edges. It nurtures patience, invites empathy, and opens your heart to joy. Each day, take a moment to say: *Thank you for walking this life with me.*

How does focusing on the things you're grateful for shift your daily experience with your dog?

**Every picture
tells a story.**
~ Unknown

Create a Memory Scrapbook

What You Need: Photos of your dog, a scrapbook and crafting materials.

What to Do: Gather photos of your favorite moments with your dog and create a scrapbook.

The Invitation: Grab your photos, markers, and memories — it's time to celebrate your life with your dog, one page at a time.

Fill your scrapbook with snapshots of adventure, joy, and everyday magic. That muddy trail hike. The nap on the couch. The goofy car ride selfie. Write little notes beside each one — a favorite moment, a funny quote, or a feeling you never want to forget.

This isn't just an art project — it's a love story told in pictures and short notes. Each image becomes a spark of laughter, a reminder of just how much your dog has shaped your days.

As you flip through the pages, inspiration grows. You'll dream up new things to do, new places to explore, more memories to capture. Your scrapbook becomes more than a keepsake — it's a living celebration of your relationship.

What thoughts or feelings come up with this activity of honoring your dog?

The mind, when
housed within a
healthful body,
possesses a glorious
sense of power.
~ Joseph Pilates

Stretching with Your Dog

What You Need: You and your dog in a comfortable, calm space.

What to Do: Perform slow gentle stretches while your dog relaxes beside you.

The Invitation: Start your day slowly, side by side. As your dog stretches — front legs long, back arched, tail high — join them. Let your body follow their lead. "Biiiiig Stretch"

Stretching together is a simple way to reconnect with your breath, your body, and your dog. It wakes up your muscles, clears your mind, and invites presence before the day begins.

Move slowly. Reach high, fold low, breathe deeply. Feel the tension soften.

Stretching is a quiet moment of connection, of honoring how your body feels, and being grateful it carried you into another day.

Let this time be soft, simple, and full of love — a gentle invitation to move through the day together with ease, awareness, and grace.

What do you notice after stretching – do your thoughts or feelings shift?

A puzzle a day
keeps your
pup's brain at play.
~ Unknown

Brain Game

What You Need: You, your dog, muffin, tennis balls, and treats.

What to Do: Play a Brain Game with your dog.

The Invitation: Tuck a treat under each ball resting in the muffin cup, then offer it to your dog. Watch as they sniff, nudge, and puzzle their way to the rewards. This simple activity taps into their natural instincts — using their nose, solving problems, and staying mentally engaged.

As they work, practice patience and encouragement. If they struggle, let empathy guide you. Learning takes time — for both of you.

This game isn't just for your dog. It reminds *you* of the value of curiosity, problem-solving, and being present. When you challenge your own mind, you sharpen focus, build resilience, and discover joy in the process.

Brain games nurture both play and growth — a shared moment of learning, laughter, and connection. The reward? Not just the treat, but the journey it took to find it.

How was this game for you and your dog?

The best seat in the house is on the floor, next to my dog.
~ Every pup parent

Lie Down on the Floor Together

What You Need: You and your dog.

What to Do: Get on the floor and relax at your dog's level.

The Invitation: Lower yourself to your dog's level. Lie down beside them. Pause. Breathe. Be present.

What does the world look like from their point of view? Notice the textures, the sounds, the way light moves across the room. Let your senses guide you.

Watch how your dog responds to your presence on the floor — their body language, their curiosity, their comfort. Being with them at their level is a powerful act of empathy — a chance to see the world through their eyes.

This simple shift in perspective may reveal ways to make their environment feel safer, softer, more welcoming. It deepens your awareness and strengthens your relationship. Connection grows by meeting someone right where they are.

What's it like to be unconditionally welcomed into your dog's space?

At the end of the day, your feet should be dirty, your hair a mess and your eyes sparkling.
~ Shanti

Daily Reflection

What You Need: You and your dog.

What to Do: In the evening, reflect with your dog about your day.

The Invitation: As the day winds down, find stillness beside your dog. Sit or lay close. Let the quiet settle in.

Reflect softly — what brought you joy today? What challenged you? What are you grateful for? Speak your thoughts aloud. Your dog listens, not for words, but for the feeling behind them — calm, steady, true.

Let this become your evening ritual. Breathe in slowly… then exhale. With each breath out, imagine tension leaving your body, sinking into the earth, carried away.

Your dog rests nearby, their presence grounding you like moonlight on water.

In this moment, there's nothing to fix, nothing to do — together, you let the day go. And, you'll begin again tomorrow.

What comes into your awareness as you and your dog gently release the day?

What we have once
enjoyed we can never
lose. All that we
love deeply becomes
a part of us.
~ Helen Keller

A Love Letter to Your Dog

What You Need: You, your dog, paper and pen.

What to Do: Write a heartful letter to your dog.

The Invitation: Take a moment to write your dog a love letter. Let the words flow — your gratitude, your favorite memories, the ways they've changed your life.

Putting pen to paper brings your emotions closer to the surface. It allows you to speak truth from the heart — to name what this relationship has given you.

Read it aloud. Your dog may not understand every word, but they'll feel your meaning. Dogs always do.

This simple act deepens your connection. It opens space for vulnerability, honesty, and love. It becomes a keepsake — a reflection of the bond you've built, the life you've shared, the love that lives between you. In writing, you remember: They are not just a pet. They are your heart's companion, your best friend — and they deserve to hear it.

Can you articulate the many feelings you have for your dog? How does it feel to express them?

Music can change the world because it can change people.
~ Ludwig von Beethoven

Create Your Dog's Music Playlist

What You Need: You, your dog and a music streaming app.

What to Do: Curate a playlist of calming music for your dog.

The Invitation: Choose calming music — soft acoustic, classical, or soundtracks made just for dogs. Play it softly. Sit together. Listen.

Notice what happens. A deep sigh. A softening of the body. The quiet settling that drifts in as the notes surround you.

Music has the power to shift energy — for both dogs and humans. It soothes the nervous system; eases tension and invites stillness. Your dog may stretch out, their breath slow and steady, fully at ease in the shared peace.

In time, the body remembers. The melodies you choose become anchors — gentle signals of safety, calm, and connection.

Let this playlist become a quiet ritual. A way to come home to yourselves, again and again, through the simple, powerful language of sound.

What do you notice within yourself and with your dog as you listen to the music?

**The beauty of the
natural world lies
in the details.**
~ Natalie Angier

Watch Nature Videos Together

What You Need: You, your dog and nature video.

What to Do: Watch videos of nature scenes with your dog.

The Invitation: Turn on a nature video. Call your dog over and explore the world — together.

Brilliant birds, ocean depths, wild landscapes — the screen becomes a window to places beyond your everyday view. As you watch, notice your dog's reactions: the tilt of their head, a paw lifted, a curious bark. Let their wonder invite your own.

Sharing this experience deepens your sense of connection — not just to your dog, but to the greater world. It's a quiet reminder that you're part of something vast, beautiful, and interconnected.

A simple video can spark curiosity, widen empathy, and inspire a sense of belonging to the wild, living world — even from your couch.

How does your worldview expand when you and your dog watch videos of far-off wild places?

May you be happy.
May you be healthy.
May you be safe.
May you live with ease.
~ Metta Meditation

LovingKindness Meditation

What You Need: You, your dog and a comfortable, quiet spot.

What to Do: With your dog beside you, practice the LovingKindness Meditation.

The Invitation: Sit quietly with your dog beside you. Take a slow breath. Close your eyes. Place your hands over your heart and silently offer yourself love and kindness.

Then, gently rest your hands on your dog. Whisper, *"I wish you love and kindness,"* and imagine that energy flowing from your hands to theirs — warm, steady, unconditional. Let it be slow. No rush. Just love, passed between two beings who know each other by heart.

Now expand that love. Let it ripple outward — to friends, to family, to strangers, to all beings — until the whole world feels wrapped in your compassion. Then, gently return that kindness back to yourself. Feel the circle complete.

This gentle practice reminds you: To live as your dog does — open-hearted and connected to all.

What shift within you as you give love and kindness to yourself and others?

When you nap
with your dog,
time slows down,
worries fade, and the
world just feels right.
~ Unknown

Nap with Your Dog

What You Need: You, your dog and soft place to rest.

What to Do: lay down with your dog for a nap.

The Invitation: Lay down beside your dog. Take a slow, deep breath. Feel their presence — steady, warm, grounding. Let their body become your anchor to the moment. Napping together is more than rest — it's comfort, connection, and trust. There's a quiet safety in being close enough to sleep side by side.

Notice how you both shift and settle. What position brings the deepest rest? Let yourself sink into the rhythm of their breath, the warmth of their body, the softness of their fur. They enjoy your company just as much as you enjoy theirs.

No words needed — only stillness. Close your eyes. Let the world fall away as you rest together, heart to heart. A nap shared in love is never just sleep — it's a gentle way to say, *I'm here. You're safe.*

How does your sleep change knowing your dog is beside you?

**The secret ingredient
is always love.**
~ Anyone who bakes

Make Homemade Dog Treats

What You Need: You, your dog, a treat recipe and its ingredients.

What to Do: Bake healthy dog treats for your dog.

The Invitation: Gather your ingredients, call your dog — it's time to bake with love.

Baking treats together is more than a recipe — it's a shared experience of care and gratitude. Let your dog sniff each ingredient, supervise your stirring, and sneak a safe lick from the bowl. This process engages your senses — the texture of the dough, the scent of peanut butter or pumpkin, the sound of laughter as flour spills. It's messy, playful, grounding — and entirely worth it.

Patience bubbles as the timer counts down. Then, the joy of giving: warm treats in hand, tail wagging in anticipation. Watch your dog's excitement as they taste the love you baked in.

These small rituals become memories, sweetened by presence and shared delight. Because sometimes, the best things are made - not with just ingredients – but with joy and togetherness.

What your dog's favorite homemade treat?

Sometimes, the best
moments in life are
the ones you don't
put into words.
~ Unknown

Movie Night

What You Need: You, your dog, a cosy spot and a dog movie.

What to Do: Curl up with your dog and watch a dog-based movie.

The Invitation: Curl up with your dog and press play on a dog-centered story. Whether it's the animated adventure of *Balto* or the emotional journey of *A Dog's Purpose*, let it be a shared escape.

Watch how your dog responds — the tilt of their head, the perk of their ears, their gaze fixed on the screen. These stories of loyalty, love, and bravery invite both of you into something tender and familiar.

Slow down. Share a simple snack. Let the world fall away for a while. Movie night becomes more than entertainment — it's a shared experience that sparks empathy, connection, and joy.
It's a gentle reminder of what matters most: being together, side by side, hearts open and full.

In the glow of the screen and the warmth of your dog beside you, let yourself simply *be*.

How does your dog respond to the dogs on the screen? What else do you notice?

**Good night,
sleep tight.
I love you.
~ Me**

Always Say Goodnight

What You Need: A bedtime routine for you and your dog.

What to Do: Before going to bed, say goodnight to your dog.

The Invitation: Before heading to bed, take a quiet moment with your dog.

Gently stroke down their back, offer a kiss on the forehead, and whisper *goodnight* with intention. Let them hear your love in every word:
You are not alone. You matter to me. I love you.

This simple ritual becomes a thread of comfort — a nightly reminder of safety, connection, and peace.

Dogs thrive on routine, and when love closes the day, they settle more easily. So do you.

As the world grows still, let this be your final offering: presence, affection, gratitude.

A peaceful end to the day…
and a soft beginning to rest.

How do you say goodnight to your dog?

Outdoor Activities

Nature becomes your classroom in these outdoor activities. Move, play and connect more deeply with your dog and the world around you.

**An early morning walk
is a blessing for the
whole day.**
~ Henry David
Thoreau

Walking with Awareness

What You Need: You, your dog and a safe walking area.

What to Do: Take your dog for a walk.

The Invitation: As you walk with your dog, slow your pace. Bring your attention to each step — the sound of paws on pavement, the bounce of ears, the rhythm of breath, yours and theirs.

Take in the world around you — the rustle of leaves, the shifting light, the scents that drift past. Let your dog lead you into presence, one moment at a time. They don't rush. They notice. Each sniff, each sound is its own experience, fully lived.

Walking mindfully together helps you step out of your busy mind and into the world as it is — simple, alive, enough. Matching your dog's pace teaches patience, expands appreciation, and reveals the quiet joy of just *being* together.

This isn't just a walk — it's a practice.
A return to the present moment, guided by the one who knows how to live it best.

How does your inner world respond to this walk?

Look deep into nature, and then you will understand everything better.

~ Albert Einstein

Blaze a New Trail

What You Need: You, your dog and an adventurous spirit.

What to Do: Visit a new trail or park with your dog.

The Invitation: Exploring new places with your dog awakens curiosity, reduces stress, and builds confidence — for both of you.

Let your dog lead the way, nose to the ground, fully engaged. As they sniff and explore, open your own senses. Notice the shifting scenery, the unfamiliar textures underfoot, the scent of new air, the sound of somewhere you've never been.

Blazing a new trail invites you to leave the familiar behind and step into wonder. Let your dog remind you how to move through the world — not with a destination in mind, but with all senses awake.

The best adventures are often found in the little things: a hidden path, a quiet clearing, a moment of awe. Step out of your comfort zone. Walk together into something new. And discover how alive the world becomes when you're willing to explore it — side by side.

What do you notice as you explore a new place?

To plant a garden is to
believe in the future.
~ AudreyHepburn

Grow a Garden

What You Need: You, your dog, dog safe plants, and a garden area or pot.

What to Do: Create a garden space and grow some plants.

The Invitation: Gardening is a mindful practice — one that calms the mind, nurtures patience, and connects you to life's quiet rhythms.

Gather dog-friendly veggies, herbs, or berries, and invite your dog to dig in beside you. Feel the soil in your hands, the scent of earth rising, the joy of planting something with intention.

Tending a garden becomes a shared ritual — a daily step into nature, a moment to slow down and notice. Watch the bees, feel the breeze, and observe the small changes that, over time, lead to something beautiful.

Create a pot or plot that welcomes pollinators and celebrates the interconnectedness of plant, animal, and human life. As your garden grows, so does your gratitude. Celebrate the harvest — and enjoy the feast together, rooted in care and shared creation.

What do you learn with this long-term activity?

The night sky is a
reminder that we are
part of something vast.
~ Unknown

Stargaze

What You Need: You, your dog, blanket and a clear night sky.

What to Do: Lay outside with your dog and observe the sky.

The Invitation: As night settles in, grab a blanket and invite your dog outside.

Stargazing invites stillness — a chance to reflect, to give thanks for the day, and gently release it. Let the quiet of the evening soothe what's restless inside you. Breathe in peace. Exhale the weight of the day.

Lie back together and look up. Notice the moon, the stars, drifting clouds. Listen — night birds call, an owl hoots in the distance, fireflies flicker like tiny lanterns around you. Smell the breeze — maybe it carries the scent of fresh grass or a nearby fire pit. Feel the shift as the heat of the day gives way to the cool hush of night.

Side by side, grounded on earth, you and your dog are part of something vast, wild, and beautifully connected. Just you, your dog, and the stars.

What do you notice as you release the day under the stars with your dog?

**Sit in silence,
what do you hear?**
~ Unknown

Listen to Nature Together

What You Need: You, your dog and quiet outdoor space.

What to Do: Sit outside in stillness with your dog.

The Invitation: Step outside with your dog and pause. Let the moment open around you — not to do, but to listen.

What catches your dog's attention? Follow their gaze, their ears. Let their curiosity guide yours.

Can you identify the sounds that surround you? Birdsong, wind through leaves, a distant car, a squirrel's chatter — nature and man-made weaving a unique soundtrack of now.

Be still. Notice which sounds bring comfort — the rhythm of your dog's breath, the gentle sweep of their tail, the quiet companionship shared without words.

Listening with your dog cultivates awareness, presence, and connection — to each other and to the living world around you. Just this moment, side by side, attuned to the wonder of what is.

What catches your dog's attention? Do you notice the same things?

**Walk as if you are
kissing the Earth
with your feet.**
~ Thich Nhat Hanh

Barefoot Walking

What You Need: You, your dog and a grassy or sandy area.

What to Do: Walk barefoot alongside your dog.

The Invitation: Step outside. Slip off your shoes. Walk with intention beside your dog.

Feel each step — toes, midfoot, heel — meeting the earth with gentle awareness. Notice the textures beneath you: the cool press of grass, the crunch of leaves, the tickle of dirt, or the sharpness of a stray pebble.

This simple act becomes a moving meditation, grounding you in your body and anchoring you to the present moment. As you walk, consider your dog's experience — how they navigate the same terrain through the pads of their feet.

Barefoot walking builds connection — not just with the earth, but with your dog. Together, you explore the world in shared awareness, one step at a time. Let your feet and theirs lead the way.

Does this activity bring you any additional awareness to how your dog may experience the world?

**You must not blame
me if I do talk
to the clouds.**
~ Henry David
Thoreau

Cloud Watching

What You Need: You, your dog and soft spot outside.

What to Do: Lay down with your dog and watch the clouds.

The Invitation: Lay back. Lock your hands behind your head. Take a deep breath — and feel your body begin to soften.

For a moment, it's just you and your dog, watching the sky. Notice the clouds — their shape, their speed, how the light plays against their edges. Let your gaze wander. Then let your imagination wake up. What do you see in the sky? A sailing ship? A dancing bear? A story waiting to be told?

Share it with your dog. Speak it aloud. They may not understand the words, but they'll feel the warmth behind them.

This quiet ritual invites stillness, creativity, and connection. In naming clouds and slowing time, you nurture presence — and create space for softness, vulnerability, and joy. Just you, your dog, and the sky — drifting, dreaming, together.

What do you notice within your body as you lay with your dog in this contemplative space?

Some people walk
in the rain,
others just get wet.
~ Roger Miller

Rainy Day Play

What You Need: You, your dog and a rainy day.

What to Do: Grab your raincoat, your dog and head outside into the rain.

The Invitation: When the raindrops start to fall, don't run for cover. Step outside with your dog and welcome the change.

Rain transforms the world — the smell of wet earth, the shimmer on leaves, the rhythm of drops hitting puddles. Notice how you and your dog move differently in this watery world.

Splash through puddles. Catch raindrops on your tongue. Let your dog lead the way in play — muddy paws, wagging tails, joy without hesitation.

Rainy day play invites spontaneity, laughter, and freedom. It's a reminder that joy isn't found only in perfect conditions — sometimes, it's in the messy, wet, and wonderfully unexpected.

Together, you learn to meet the moment with open hearts, no matter the weather. Dance in the drizzle. Celebrate the storm, soaked in joy.

What's it like for you to play in the rain?

**Scent is the strongest
tie to memory.**
~ Unknown

Sniffy Walk

What You Need: You, your dog and an open mind and extra time.

What to Do: Let your dog take the lead on our walk.

The Invitation: On a sniffy walk, you're not setting the pace — your dog is. Giving your dog control fosters trust, honors their instincts, and supports their confidence.

Follow their nose. Let them linger, backtrack, pause, and explore. Notice what draws their attention. What scent has them rooted to one spot, breathing it in with full-body focus?

This is more than a walk — it's a sensory adventure, a shared exploration of the world through their eyes and nose. As you follow, stay curious. What are they discovering? What are *you* learning as you slow down and tune in?

A sniffy walk reminds you that sometimes, the best journeys are the ones where you surrender control — and simply enjoy the path your dog leads you down.

What do you notice when you let your dog lead?

**The quieter you become,
the more you can hear.**
~ Ram Dass

Mindful Listening Walk

What You Need: You, your dog and a peaceful walking path.

What to Do: Take a walk with your dog.

The Invitation: As you walk with your dog, tune into the sounds around you. Start close — the soft jingle of their tags, the rhythm of your footsteps, the whisper of your breath. Then, slowly expand your awareness. Can you hear birdsong nearby? A dog barking in the distance? The hum of life all around you? Try to sense how far away each sound is.

Dogs do this naturally — their ears twitching, heads turning, fully attuned to the world. When your dog pauses to listen, pause with them. Stay curious. Mindful listening sharpens focus and quiets the mind. It anchors you to the present, inviting you into a deeper relationship with your environment — and with your dog.

Walking becomes more than movement — it becomes a meditation on sound, and the unseen world always humming just beneath the surface.

If taking the same path, do the sounds change with the seasons or even the time of day?

Not all those who
wander are lost.
~ J. R. R. Tolkien

Take a New Route

What You Need: You, your dog and an adventurous spirit.

What to Do: Take a different route for your daily walk.

The Invitation: Instead of your usual path, go in the opposite direction — explore your neighborhood with fresh eyes.

Notice what changes when the familiar is seen from a new angle. What details pop out? A flower you've never noticed, a new scent your dog finds fascinating, the way the light falls differently.

Changing your routine adds variety, enrichment, and a renewed sense of discovery — for both you and your dog. New paths spark curiosity, awaken awareness, and invite you to be more fully present.

Your dog will lead the way with nose to the ground, following new trails of scent and sound. Let yourself be pulled into their excitement. Share in the small joys of noticing something new — together.

What shifts with the new perspective?

There's a sunrise
and a sunset every
single day, and
they're absolutely free.
~ Jo Walton

Sunrise Meditation

What You Need: You, your dog and an early morning wake up.

What to Do: Watch the sun rise together.

The Invitation: Rise early and greet the day with your dog by your side. Let the stillness of morning wrap around you. Sunrises invite you to pause — to breathe, to listen, to simply *be*.

Whisper, *"Thank you for this day together."* Let it be a quiet blessing — for your dog, for yourself, and for the unfolding day.

Notice the soft light stretching across the sky, the hush giving way to birdsong, the retreat of shadows as warmth and color slowly return.

There is something sacred in beginning the day with intention — grounded in the moment and guided by gratitude.

As you and your dog step into the new day, let your pace be slow, your heart open, your awareness sharp. Each day is a gift.

Is there a reverence that emerges as you and your dog start your day watching the sunrise?

Nothing says adventure
like the smell of
wet dog.
~ Unknown

Explore Water Together

What You Need: You, your dog, and safe body of water.

What to Do: Explore water together with your dog.

The Invitation: Water invites joy. Jump in with your dog. Toss a toy, paddle together, or simply watch them leap and splash with delight.

Feel how the water lightens you, makes movement easier, laughter quicker. On a warm day, nothing soothes like a cool dip — for both body and spirit.

After the fun, pause. Float, sit, or lay near the water's edge. Let stillness settle in. Feel the grounding effect of water — calming, centering, connecting you both.

In these moments, you and your dog are simply present. No rush. No agenda. Just nature, movement, and the shared rhythm of happiness and rest.

Let the water carry you — closer to your dog, to yourself, and to the moment you're living in together.

How does being water shift your inner world?

**To appreciate the
beauty of a snowflake,
it's necessary to stand
out in the cold.**
~ Aristotle

Snow Day

What You Need: You, your dog and a snowy day.

What to Do: Bundle up and go outside in the snow together.

The Invitation: Snow days invite you to pause and experience the world with fresh eyes. Explore the hush and sparkle of the snowy landscape.

Notice how sound softens under a blanket of white, how light bounces off each flake. Watch how your dog responds — bounding with joy and zoomies, or tiptoeing out, skeptical and swift. Honor their reaction — and your own.

Whether you're romping through snowdrifts, making snow angels, or simply watching from the window, stay present to what unfolds.

Feel the snow in your hands, notice its texture — wet and heavy or dry and glittering like diamonds. Let the cold awaken your senses. Let the moment be enough — just you and your dog, embracing the magic of winter, however it arrives.

What comes into your awareness as you and your dog experience a snow day?

Appendix – Dive Deeper

Within this Appendix are additional information and activities for you about some of the exercises listed in this book.

Page 2 PAWS

- PAWS for Mindful Connection

Page 11 I See You

- I See You Blessing

Page 13 Doga Yoga

- Yoga Routine

Page 21 Picnic time, Page 55 Mindful Mealtime, Page 97 Grow A Garden

- Dog Safe Fruits and Veggies

Page 23 Breathwork

Page 53 Doggie Meditation

Page 81 Lovingkindness Meditation

Page 85 Make Homemade Dog Treats

Page 2 PAWS

PAWS for Mindful Connection

This exercise is a key component of Mindfulness Practice. With just a little pause to tune-in to your experience in this moment, you can respond in the most appropriate way to your current situation or experience. Take one minute to do a mindful check-in. Use the following to help you take a PAWS and connect with yourself:

P – **Pause** – come to stillness, stop

A – **Air** - Take a breath

W – **Wonder -** What am I thinking/saying and feeling? How is my body responding? What's my energy like? What is happening around me?

S – **Step forward** - Resume interactions with greater awareness and understanding

Page 11: I See You

I See You Blessing

We all long to be seen and acknowledged. This blessing is an opportunity for you to slow down and see the Other Person or Being you are interacting with. It deepens your ability to be present and gifts someone else your attention and focus. This is a wonderful activity to do with the clerk at the store, your child, your boss, your dog, or with the person in the mirror.

- Meet the being's eyes – make eye contact
- In your head, say: "I see you."
- Blink or otherwise break eye contact

You don't even have to smile at the person, simply by intentionally saying the words in your head, it shifts how you are engaging with them. You are acknowledging and honoring their presence. You can substitute "Namaste" if you prefer. Namaste means the love and light within me sees the love and light within you.

Page 13: Dog Yoga

This gentle yoga routine supports connecting mind and body while reducing stress. Invite your dog to join you.

---

1. Mountain Pose

Quiets mind, engages core muscles, grounding

- Stand feet hip width apart
- Shoulders back, arms at the side, palms forward
- 3 slow breaths

---

2. Standing – Forward Bend

Stretches hamstrings, lower back, shoulders arms

- Inhale, raise arms above head
- Exhale, bend forward at waist
- Settle into fold, grasping arms at opposite elbows
- 5 slow breaths

---

3. Standing Wide Leg, Forward Fold

Stretches legs, hamstrings, shoulders, arms

- Inhale, raise arms above head
- Exhale, dropping arms, bend forward at waist
- Swing arms behind back & lift arms up as comfortable
- 5 slow breaths
- Return to Mountain Pose

124

4. Half Moon Pose

Whole Body Stretch

- Bring arms above head, arms parallel
- Side bend to left, 5 breaths
- Come to center, breathe
- Side bend to right, 5 breaths
- Return to Mountain Pose

5. Cow and Cat Pose

Stretches lower back and shoulders, slows breathing

- Go to mat, on heads and knees – neutral spine
- Inhale and tip hipbones up into Cow Pose
- Exhale, round back into Cat Pose
- Return to neutral spine
- Repeat sequence 5 breaths

6. Child's Pose

Stretches legs, lower back, spine, opens hips

- From hands and knees, gently sit back onto heels
- Fold torso over thighs
- Stretch arms in front of you, resting on mat
- Drop head to mat
- 5 breaths, emphasizing exhale

Page 21: Picnic Time, Page 55: Mindful Mealtime, Page 97: Grow a Garden

Many of the foods that you eat can be enjoyed by dogs. However, remember that "table scraps" are usually not the best choice for our dogs. The foods we consume typically have additional salt, sugar or seasonings added to them that makes it a poor choice for our dogs. Mindfully preparing food specifically for your dog is a healthier choice. Fruits and veggies are great foods to add variety to your dog's diet. They are simple foods that you can enjoy together.

Dog Safe Fruits and Veggies to Grow and Eat

apples - apricots - avocados (meat only - bananas - blackberries - blueberries - cantaloupe - canary melon - cherries (remove pit) - clementines - coconut - grapefruit - honeydew melon - kiwi - mangos (remove pit) - nectarines (remove pit) - oranges - papaya - peaches (remove pit) - pears - pineapple (meat only) plums - pomegranate - raspberries - strawberries - tomatoes - watermelon - alfalfa sprouts - asparagus - anise - beets - broccoli - Brussels sprouts - carrots - cauliflower - celery - chicory - corn - courgette - cucumber - garlic (in small amounts) - green beans - ginger - green/red leaf lettuce - kale - kelp - mushrooms (only human friendly kind) - parsnips - peas - potatoes - pumpkin - romaine - spinach - sugar snap peas - sweet peppers - sweet potatoes - yams - yellow beans

Be aware of the foods that are harmful to your dog. Avoid feeding your dog:

- xylitol (common ingredient in peanut butter)
- alcohol
- onions & onion powder
- caffeine
- large amounts of garlic
- chocolate & candy
- high fat foods (like bacon grease)
- cooked bones
- grapes and raisins
- coffee
- salt
- pits & seeds of any fruit
- tomato plants - leaves and stem

Think about all of the ingredients used to create the food item; many gravies, meat rubs, casseroles, etc have several seasonings & ingredients that could hurt your dog.

Page 23: Breathwork with Your Dog

Breathwork Techniques

There are many different breathing techniques that offer strategies for pain and stress management, better focus, and increased oxygen intake. Breathwork gives you the chance to pause, take a breath, and reengage with your life. Notice that your dog also regulates their emotions through their breath.

Abdominal breathing/Belly breaths – Immediately slows your heart rate and calms your mind and body.

- Place one hand on your chest and one over your stomach
- Breathe deeply in through your nose so your stomach inflates and exhale through your mouth while your stomach contracts

4 x 4 Breaths – Slows your heart rate and calms your mind and body

- 4 count in, 4 count hold, 4 count release, 4 count wait

The Counting Breaths – This is the simplest form of breath exercise.

- Count your breaths. Each time you exhale, add a count.

Cooling Breath - Good for those times when you are hot. Whether that's physically overheated or feeling the heat of anger, reversing your breathing pattern will literally cool you off.

- Roll your tongue or purse your lips
- Inhale through your mouth
- Close your mouth
- Exhale through nose

Complete 5 rounds of breathing

Page 53: Doggie Meditation

Doggie Meditation

This meditation is for you and your dog. Find a quiet place. Sit or lay beside your dog so you are level with your dog. Gently and slowly use all of your senses to connect with your dog.

Sight: Look at your dog, make eye contact. Starting at their head, notice the details about the appearance of your dog. nose to tail.

Touch: Run your fingers through their fur, front to back, top to bottom. What textures do you feel?

Sound: Can you hear them? What sounds do you associate with your dog?

Smell: Bury your nose in their fur. What do you smell? What other smells do you associate with your dog?

Taste: Give your dog a kiss. Thank them for being in your life.

Page 85: Homemade Dog Treats

Peanut Butter Dog Treats

Ingredients:

- 2 ¼ Cup Whole Wheat Flour
- 1 Cup Oatmeal
- ¼ Cup Peanut Butter
- 1 TBSP Vegetable Oil
- 1 Cup Water

Combine peanut butter, oil, and water. Add flour and oatmeal. Mix well with blender. Lightly flour hands and knead dough for 30 seconds. Roll out to 1/4' thickness. Use a pizza cutter to slice strip of dough, then cut again into tiny bite-size pieces or use a cookie cutter for cute shapes.

Bake at 350 degrees for 25 minutes.

Let treats completely cool before serving to your dog.

Remember, when baking or cooking anything, you add a magical ingredient called love to the recipe.

Sources

ASPCA, "People Foods to Avoid Feeding Your Pets." https://www.aspca.org/pet-care/animal-poison-control/people-foods-avoid-feeding-your-pets

Cronkleton, Emily. "Breathwork" https://www.healthline.com (August 15, 2018)

Jurica, Vicki and Laub, Melissa. *Ally Dog Team Training Workbook.* USA. Ally Dog Training Program LLC 2021

Keltner, Dacher "Importance of Touch" https://www.greatergood.berkeley.edu (January 10,2021)

Peanut Butter Homemade Dog Treats recipe, courtesy of Bakery & Co.. Owner Vicki Jurica

Portions of the content were developed with the assistance of ChatGPT, an AI language model created by OpenAI, used to support editing.

About the Author

Vicki Jurica is Certified as a Hypnotist, Trauma-Informed Life Coach, Mindfulness Teacher and lifelong animal advocate. A dedicated shelter volunteer and former co-founder of an organization pairing sexual assault survivors with rescue dogs for healing, Vicki is passionate about the transformative power of the human-animal bond. As an artist and creator of multiple books and affirmation card decks, she inspires others to embrace their own healing journeys through the wisdom and love of animals.

Additional publications: *Mutt & Mindfulness* Card Deck, *Resource Reminders* Card Deck, *Barkery & Co. Cookbook, and Mindful Resilience* (available through Amazon and Etsy)

www.tealpaws.com
www.meadowlarkhypnosis.com